Professor Birdsong's

Weird Criminal Law Stories

Leonard Birdsong
Winghurst Publications

Professor Birdsong's Weird Criminal Law Stories
by Leonard Birdsong

Winghurst Publications
1969 S. Alafaya Trail / Suite 303
Orlando, FL 32828-8732
www.BirdsongsLaw.com
lbirdsong@barry.edu

Disclaimer:
The facts that are recounted in the stories in this volume are true and in the public domain, as best as Professor Birdsong can determine from his research of court documents, newspapers, and wire services. The author's commentaries on these stories are his own views and opinions and do not reflect the official policy or position of any Law school, Law firm or other organization with which the author may be affiliated. The opinions provided herein are not intended to malign or defame any religion, ethnic group, club, organization, company, individual or anyone or anything. The author further covenants and represents that the work contains no matter that will incite prejudice, amount to an invasion of privacy, be libelous, obscene or otherwise unlawful or which infringe upon any proprietary interest at common law, trademark, trade secret, patent or copyright. The author is the sole proprietor of the work and all parts thereof.

Cover graphics:
Copyright Albund | Dreamstime.com
Copyright Eric Basir | Dreamstime.com

Book cover design:
Rik Feeney / Rik@PublishingSuccessOnline.com

TABLE OF CONTENTS

Introduction

Professor Leonard Birdsong lives in Orlando, Florida where he teaches Criminal Law, White Collar Crime, Evidence, and Immigration Law. He received his Juris Doctor degree from the Harvard Law School and his Bachelor's degree from Howard University. He has written many scholarly legal pieces since joining the legal academy. This is not one of those scholarly pieces! This volume of Weird Criminal Law Stories is written just for fun and enjoyment.

Professor Birdsong is proud of his legal career which included his work as an attorney with the law firm of Baker & Hostetler. Later he served as a diplomat with the State Department with various postings in Nigeria, Germany, and the Bahamas. Professor Birdsong also worked as a federal prosecutor, first as an Assistant United States Attorney for the District of Columbia, and later as a

Special Assistant United States Attorney for the U.S. Virgin Islands.

After leaving government service, Professor Birdsong was in private practice in Washington, D.C., where he specialized in trial work ranging from criminal defense work to political asylum matters.

While in practice he also did on-air TV legal analysis work for Fox News, CNN, Court TV, BET TV News, and for W*USA Channel 9 in Washington, D.C. During this same period, he also produced and hosted several radio talk programs in the Washington, D.C., and Baltimore areas. Currently, Professor Birdsong is occasionally invited to appear as a legal commentator on Fox News, MSNBC, Fox Radio, and CBS Radio.

Although he has been involved in serious criminal law work over the years as a prosecutor, a defense attorney, and a law professor, Professor Birdsong knows that it is good to stayed grounded. This means often taking time to look at the many funny and weird criminal law stories that crop up around the United States and the world. He believes we should not always take criminal law so seriously and instead, just have a good laugh at some of the silly foibles of dumb criminals and their crimes. That is why several years ago he began to collect and edit from the wire services and news the type of weird and funny criminal law stories that appear in this volume.

Professor Birdsong hopes that you will get a few good laughs or at least, some chuckles from this collection of weird criminal law stories and his "snarky" commentary accompanying each of them.

Enjoy!

Weird Criminal Law Stories

CHAPTER ONE

Weird but true criminal law stories from around the United States.

This first chapter is comprised of some of Professor Birdsong's favorite weird criminal law stories from 2010. They are all true.

Findlay, OH: This really is a weird one. A woman called Findlay police one recent weekend to complain that her husband claimed that her daughter -- his stepdaughter -- had performed oral sex on him and was far better at it than her mom. Police made note of this crime against humanity but had to tell the woman it actually did not violate any part of the penal code.

That's funny....seems there may have been a violation of some "penal" code!

Lynnwood, WA: A man accidentally shot himself in the testicles at a hardware store in Lynnwood. He was carrying his pistol in the waistband of his pants on a Sunday, and it accidentally went off, police said. It was reported the man's leg and foot were also injured.

Is his manhood still intact? Inquiring minds would like to know!

Toledo, OH: It has been reported that Ohio strippers are doing their part to help out victims of the spring 2010 Midwest tornados. Marilyn's on Monroe in Toledo will donate all the door charges from its "Lap Dances for Northwestern Ohio" event to those impacted by the tornados. This same strip club raised $1,000 with its "Lap Dances for Haiti" earlier in the year.

Whip it baby, whip it right, whip it baby, whip it all night...

Raleigh, NC: A campus religious leader is allegedly unhappy about a study at Duke University that invites female students to attend parties where they can buy sex toys. The News & Observer of Raleigh reported that the director of the Duke Catholic Center has lodged a complaint with researchers.

Vibrator haters... BZZZZZZZZZZZZZ....

Connecticut: "Drop the Bazooka!" read the headline. A New York newspaper reported there appears to be a crime wave in Connecticut -- sticky fingered thieves are stealing chewing gum at stores around the state. In one of the biggest heists, a 21-year old man was charged with shoplifting about $800 worth of gum in Stratford, Bridgeport and Fairfield. Police believe the "gum thieves" want something they can sell quickly and is hard to trace.

Nothing like a good chew.

ARKANSAS: An enraged Arkansas man arguing with his drunken son tossed a handgun to the son, dared him to "pull the trigger" – and was shot dead. Zachary Bowers, 22, told police: "Dad threw the gun in my hand and told me to pull the trigger. I pulled the trigger and shot him." The young Bowers was charged with murder.

Bang, you're dead. Shame..... So sad.

Hutchinson, KS: Kids, don't try this one in court. A Kansas defense attorney who wanted to illustrate for jurors the meaning of "imminent threat" pulled out a hand grenade in a Hutchinson court, pulled the pin and put it down on the prosecutor's table. The lawyer said the grenade was a dud. His client was a woman accused of forgery and theft. She claimed a co-defendant had threatened to kill her dog and harm her daughter if she didn't take part in the scheme. The lawyer may face charges.

Ka-Boom! That stunt sure blew up in his face!

Maine: What a "dopey" way to pay one's legal bills! Stephen Petrocelli, a resident of the state of Maine, was arrested for allegedly growing marijuana in his house. He was doing so in order to get enough money to pay off the attorney who had defended him in a different drug case in Missouri. Petrocelli, who had recently moved to Maine from Missouri, was arrested when his probation officer did a home inspection.

Yep, a real dope!

Los Alamitos, CA: Drunken driver Matthew Van McDaniel of Los Alamitos was handed a nine year prison sentence for crashing his Mercedes Benz through the gates of a prison and then bloodying the nose of a corrections officer trying to restrain him. McDaniel's attorney said that his client "looks forward to period of self reflection."

Seems like 9 years provides that perfect period to self reflect...

Missouri: A Missouri woman who attempted to run down a man with her car was arrested and then used her one phone call from jail to call and taunt her alleged victim. It is reported that a police officer who overheard the telephone call described it as "pretty ugly." Witnesses at the scene of the crime reported that the woman appeared under the influence of drugs.

The headline asked: "Is there a charge of assault and mockery?"

Los Angeles, CA: Lance Ito, the judge in the O.J. Simpson murder case of several years ago, recently sentenced a defendant to 12 years in another strange case. Rueben Hernandez was arrested after police pursued him on a high speed chase after he had bought six properties using fake Social Security information. At the home he was staying police found voodoo dolls dunked head first in cups of water with pins in their eyes. The dolls bore the names of the prosecutor and the detectives on the case.

Sounds like Reuben do that voodoo that he do so well.....but it didn't work!

Cleveland, OK: Jail officials in Cleveland County dress inmates in hot pink shirts and yellow and white striped pants that some complain make them look more like clowns than prisoners. Jail officials say the new outfits make it easier to find escapees.

Oh my...

Wenatchee, WA: Speaking of prisoners, here's another one. In Washington state a prison inmate smuggled in a cigarette lighter, rolling paper, a golf ball size bag of tobacco, another small bag of marijuana, a small smoking pipe, a bottle of tattoo ink and eight tattoo needles -- all in his rectum. The prison contraband was found after a worker found a plastic bag and duct tape in the toilet and questioned the man.

Did they question him about how his rectum got so large?

Riverton, WY: Police say a man suspected of stealing a bottle of Schnapps from a Wyoming grocery store did not have the best escape route planned. Riverton police say the 26 year old ran out of the store after grabbing the bottle of liquor and a package of cough drops and hid in a nearby building -- which happened to be the town police station. Police say the man then ran out of the police station, but not before a dispatcher had spied him on the station's surveillance camera and alerted officers. The man, who police say was drunk, was caught soon after.

Drunken dummy!

Wisconsin: There is a report that a Wisconsin man convicted of trying to steal dirty diapers from a stranger's home is not getting "pampered." The 20 year old man, convicted of possession of burglary tools, was sentenced to 30 months of probation and a psychosexual exam.

Dirty diapers -- Phew!

Darien, CT: In early June 2010, a naked man on the highway, yelling that he was Jesus, sparked a five car wreck on northbound I-95 in Darien, injuring three people and slowing traffic for nearly six hours.

WWJD?

West Virginia: The headline read: "This educator has no class." It is reported that a West Virginia substitute teacher was told on by her third grade students for drinking in the classroom. Sabina Prado, 50, was removed from the school for allegedly being drunk in public and consuming alcohol on school property.

Wow! How tough was that third grade class that she needed booze to face them?

Massachusetts: A first grader in Massachusetts stumbled upon three bags of heroin near his bus stop and took them to school where he gave them to classmates. Not knowing what they had, they handed the $1400 worth of dope to their teachers.

These kids did say "no to drugs."

Nevada: A police detective in Nevada was arrested for burglary and assault for allegedly harassing political candidates. He turned himself into police and then issued a press release regarding his own arrest. David Boruchowitz, who is also a county sheriff's office spokesman, included his own booking photo in the release.

It's called one stop policing.

Union, SC: It appears this senior citizen may have had a bad hair day. Police said they caught 72 year old Sandra Powell speeding down the highway at more than 100 mph. The police report indicates "she was upset because she was late for a hair appointment."

ZOOM! ZOOM!

Ohio: An Ohio woman whose teen grandson plowed her SUV into a Verizon Wireless store paid her cell phone bill before she backed the vehicle out. Seems the woman had been on her way to the store one Thursday in June when her 16 year old grandson, who was behind the wheel, hit the gas pedal instead of the brake and crashed through the windows.

Tinkle. Tinkle. Tinkle.

South Brunswick, NJ: A New Jersey man charged with DUI believed he needed some liquid courage before going before the judge in his case. He had a few more drinks before driving to his court date, and of course, crashed as he made a turn. Police say he now faces two DUI charges. When questioned as to whether he had been drinking John Dematteo allegedly told police officials he was so anxious about his court appearance that he consumed some vodka.

HIC....

Columbus, OH: Sometimes one wishes to eat their words -- this next one is such a case. Police in Columbus say Lois Harvey while in line in a bank handed a teller a note demanding cash. Immediately thereafter Harvey noticed a police officer standing right behind her in the line. She quickly grabbed back the note, ran out to the street, and swallowed it. When she coughed it up on the sidewalk, the officer arrested her.

A bank robbery gone bad... how foolish.

Charles County, MD: A Maryland man called 911 and spun a tale about how he had been robbed at gunpoint -- so he could get a ride home. When the Charles County police pointed out the foolishness of his story, he admitted that he made it up. He further told police he wanted a ride, but his cell phone had no more minutes and the only number he could dial was 911.

Moron!

Pennsylvania: Police arrested a man who threatened his girlfriend with a meat cleaver after they got into an argument over the massive BP oil spill in the Gulf of Mexico. The woman, who was holding the couple's baby, was not hurt.

Yes, yes, we know...he wanted a split decision.

San Antonio, TX: Officials in San Antonio ordered a lingerie shop to get a food permit because they sell edible underwear. Not only does this mean a $230 annual fee, the shop is now subject to regular health inspections. The owners say the edible panties are purely a novelty.

YUM YUM!

Middle Township, NJ: Lawrence Walsh, 24, of Middle Township, called police to say he had been robbed at a convenience store. However, police say Walsh was actually just mad because he had been sold fake cocaine.

The nerve!

Wisconsin: Wisconsin state police had to lay down tire spikes to stop a runaway truck hauling energy drinks after the driver fell asleep at the wheel. The move was a last ditch effort after troopers leaned on their horns and shouted over loud speakers for miles as the truck barreled down the highway with the slumbering driver behind the wheel.

TOOT! TOOT!

Alabama: An Alabama geometry teacher got a visit from the Secret Service when he used the example of assassinating President Obama to teach his class the concept of how one measures angles. Investigators did not detain the teacher, but school officials were quick to say the teacher exhibited "extremely poor judgment." No word on whether he will keep his job.

He must have been a Republican....

Baltimore, MD: The headline read: "CSI Meets Lassie." Residents of an upscale condominium are voting on a plan to gather the DNA of every resident's dog to identify the perpetrator who is leaving piles of poop on the grounds. Each dog owner would be charged $50 to cover the cost of the tests, a proposal that one resident described as worthy of a "Seinfeld" episode.

Not that there is anything wrong with that!

Oakland, CA: Eighty one parole violators showed up to claim $200 and amnesty in May in Oakland, but their only prize was a trip back to jail. The Department of Corrections sent letters -- from a fictitious "amnesty director" -- to parolees who had cut off their ties with their parole officers.

Very tricky, but effective.... Criminals can be so stupid...

Buffalo, NY: A Buffalo man was arrested after he called cops to report that two teenagers had broken into his garage to steal his pot plants. Police investigators discovered 51 plants growing there. The teens were arrested on burglary charges while the homeowner faces a drug rap.

Senior Stupido!

Philadelphia, PA: a Philly woman on the run from police hid from them inside a coffin at a funeral home. The woman had escaped while being transported between police stations, and was caught by a funeral director who found her in the casket. Nicole April Kelly, 19, ended up being held without bail on escape charges.

Houdini she wasn't...

Vermont: A man who spent 19 years in jail for a fatal DWI car wreck was arrested a month after being freed -- for a DWI car wreck. Douglas Gardner, 54, was caught in Vermont after he crashed a car he allegedly had stolen. He had previously been convicted of DWI in 1976, 1977, 1983, 1985, 1989 and 1991.

This old school drunken driver needs to be in jail.

Minnesota: Talk about poor witness protection. Police in Minnesota accidentally placed a murder suspect and the witness who implicated him in the same courtroom holding cell. Not surprisingly, the witness who was jailed in a separate case, suffered a serious beating. Court officials say a computer error led to the mistake.

Either that or the clerk did it to have some fun....

Ansonia, CT: The town of Ansonia agreed to pay the legal bills of a police officer acquitted of charges he stole a garden hose from the police department. The jury found Officer Mustafa Salahuddin not guilty. He promptly sent his legal bill of $63,015.31 to the city which, after deliberation agreed to pay up.

A $63,000 legal bill for a misdemeanor crime! He must have retained Alan Dershowitz and the dream team to represent him.

Lincoln, NE: The headline read: "Nebraska cops believe they have flushed out the toilet paper bandit." The thief who masked his face by winding toilet paper around his head held up a store in Lincoln in April, 2010. He fled with an undisclosed amount of money, but left a clue -- a prescription pill bottle. Police arrested the suspect in mid-May.

They're stupid! That's why police catch them.

Georgia: We have learned that police in Georgia have finally stopped a pair of gospel singers who allegedly had broken into several churches and stolen $100,000 worth of musical equipment. Deshawn Rico and Rico Pionegro Blackshear, both 28, are believed to have burglarized a total of nine churches. Police report that they found the stolen musical equipment in both men's homes and cars.

They may have sung the gospel but they sure didn't live the gospel.

Missoula, MT: A Missoula woman who just got out of jail for stealing a police scooter, was arrested the next day for trying to steal a police car, according to a police report. She allegedly jumped into the car when the officers left it to make a traffic stop.

If at first you don't succeed, try, try again...

Waterloo, IA: Wendi Mae Mingus, 45, a hospital patient is accused of walking out of Allen Memorial Hospital in Waterloo while still attached to a heart monitor. She wanted to go out for a smoke, but staffers wouldn't allow it -- so she left on her own with the $1,000 wireless monitor still attached.

Can we say she stole their heart, yuk, yuk, yuk....

Hawkinsville, GA: A prank by 16 Georgia high school seniors will leave them facing felony charges as well as being barred from attending their graduation. Evidence shows that the "Hawkinsville 16" turned loose a gaggle of chickens in the school's hallway and put sardines in the school's air vents.

Cluck, Cluck...

Northampton, MA: A 20 year old woman was given a traffic citation for running down Lord Jesus Christ -- in a crosswalk! Police who responded to the accident, checked the 50 year old victim's identification and confirmed that this was truly his name. He suffered only minor injuries.

We know, we know...the devil made her do it!

Ohio: A 20 year old man in Ohio was sentenced to three years in prison for tattooing the letter A on the rear end of a 19 month old baby girl. The baby was not his. The child had been left in the care of Lee Dietrick when the baby's mother went to visit a friend who was in the hospital.

What an ass....

Pennsylvania: The headline read: "Her disability didn't prevent her from taking a pole position." Christina Gamble, a Pennsylvania waitress, who was receiving worker's compensation payment for a back injury was arrested on fraud charges after she was caught working in a topless club. Private investigators spotted her pole dancing at C.R. Fanny's Gentleman's Club while reaping about $27,000 in disability benefits.

Jiggle, jiggle and pay it all back...

Tennessee: A man who stole some cases of beer from a gas station returned a few minutes later to exchange them because the beer was warm. The clerk told police that she was in the back restocking and discovered the cases missing when she came back up front. The man returned a few minutes later and when the suspicious clerk asked if he had paid for the beer, he fled the store.

ZOOOM...

Alabama: Police in Alabama found a burglar who had broken into a veterinary clinic passed out inside after he had injected himself with animal tranquilizer while watching pornography on a computer. Officials say

Roman Angel Salinas was lucky -- if he had taken any more of the drug it would have killed him.

Almost OD in a vet clinic -- get a life loser!

Wisconsin: Here is another loser. When a pregnant Wisconsin woman went into labor and asked her boyfriend to drive her to the hospital, he beat her up and stole her money to buy beer. The woman was not seriously hurt and the baby was born without trouble. The boyfriend, Michael Vinson was charged with assault.

Yet, another loser!

Long Island, NY: A woman parked her SUV at a Long Island Department of Motor Vehicle office, recently. Apparently she forgot the vehicle sported a fake license plate. A sharp eyed DMV employee noticed the plate and called police who arrested the owner.

D'OH!

Memphis, TN: A Memphis mother called police to report that she caught her son stealing prescription drugs from her bra in a dresser drawer. The mother of accused drug abuser Charlie Boyd, 28, said she had attempted to hide her prescription Xanax pills from him. Police said they found 22 pills in his socks, and drug paraphernalia in his room.

Both mother and son are weird!

Columbus, OH: Could it be? Robin Hood lives! Police say a bandit robbed a bank in Columbus and as he ran away encountered a mother and daughter window shopping. He stopped, gave them each a $100 bill, assured them the money was real and resumed running.

Where was Friar Tuck?

Lowell, MA: A DMV clerk in Lowell was arrested for hacking into the state computer and clearing her own driving record of $1,400 in parking fines. Judy Coughlin did it so she could renew her car registration, police stated.

Her next parking space will be in jail.

Pennsylvania: The big question is -- what happened to the rest of him? Crews cleaning up the banks of Pennsylvania's Shenango River discovered a prosthetic leg, with a shoe still attached, among the 21 tons of trash they collected. Officials have recovered about 800,000 pounds of refuse from the river over the years, much of it illegally dumped scrap steel.

Has a one legged man been reported missing lately?

Boulder, CO: A Colorado lawyer has offered his services for free to any one arrested for smoking pot on 4/20. Rob Corry is a major medical marijuana advocate and said it was his honor to defend people's First Amendment rights on the annual day celebrating toking up.

Did you know that 4/20 is also Hitler's birthday?

New Haven, CT: New Haven police do not double as taxi drivers, but that did not stop Quandria Bailey, 28, from dialing 911 six times to request a ride from a nightclub back to her Meriden home. She was charged with six counts of misuse of 911. She posted a $1,000 bond and is scheduled to appear in court.

Bet alcohol had something to do with this.

Norco, CA: A California community wants to put the brakes on a pot peddler on wheels. Stewart Hauptman has been selling medical marijuana out of a souped up, 1985 motor home, and the city of Norco wants him to stop. Hauptman said he sells pot to old people outside of clinics. "These are not young kids who go out and get stoned," he told the LA Times "These are older people, some dying of cancer."

The community is afraid of becoming Narco, California.

Winona, MN: The headline shouted "The barf was worse than the bite!" Police in Minnesota say an 18 year old has a good excuse for crashing his car into a utility pole -- his dog threw up on him. An officer found the vehicle unattended against the pole, and witnesses said they saw a man leaving the area with a beagle. The teenager apparently left with his best friend because he does not have insurance or a driver's license. But he called police about four hours later to confess.

We sincerely hope the beagle feels better now.

Seattle, WA: Could the problem have been that they were playing for both teams. Three bisexual men have filed suit in Seattle against the Gay Softball World Series, claiming they were not allowed to play because they were not gay enough. the league argues that as a private organization, it is allowed to set its own membership rules.

OMG!

Washington state: A former cocaine smuggler was arrested for running a bestiality farm for tourists. Authorities seized dogs, horses, pet mice and thousands of items of bestial and child pornography at the wooded compound near the Canadian border, where Douglas Spink allegedly allowed a 51-year-old British tourist to have sex with dogs.

Bet the dogs did not like the sex...

New Hampshire: Two employees of a New Hampshire town are facing disciplinary action for grabbing 50 cases of expired beer out of the municipal landfill for themselves. Officials say it amounts to theft because anything that goes into the landfill becomes property of the town.

It was probably skunky beer anyway!

Arlington, MA: A crook broke into the home of Harvard Professor Roy Glauber and walked off with his Nobel Prize in physics. Police caught Stephen Beaulieu because he allegedly left a food stamp receipt behind. "Clearly, the victim and the alleged perpetrator in this case are on opposite ends of the IQ spectrum, " said Arlington Police Chief Frederick Ryan. The prize, however, is still missing.

Who would buy an unearned Nobel Prize in Physics? Maybe, someone up the street at MIT?

Boise, ID: A 74 year old woman in Boise was arrested after allegedly pouring mayonnaise into a library drop box, and she is being investigated for at least 10 other condiment related crimes around the town. Joy Cassidy was picked up moments after pulling into the drive-through and allegedly dumping a jar of mayo in the drop box. Library employees had reported finding books in the drop box covered in corn syrup and ketchup.

One question: WHY??

Fostoria, OH: This lady went to the top -- which was her first mistake. An Ohio prostitute was arrested after soliciting a prospective customer -- who turned out to be the chief of police. When Catherine Tate approached a parked car in Fostoria and told Chief John McGuire, she had what he needed, he whipped out his badge. She was sentenced to 15 days in jail.

OOOOOPS...

Indiana: Perhaps, there is no need to jail this perpetrator -- this may have been punishment enough. Police hunting a man suspected of running a meth lab found him hiding neck-deep in a pool filled with manure at an Indiana pig farm. After police dragged him out of the feces, he became combative and had to be stun-gunned.

Who wouldn't be combative after being pulled from a pool of pig poop!

Riverside/San Bernadino, CA: The headline read: "California Cops extinguish an odd crime spree." A 45 year old man was arrested for allegedly stealing 45 fire hydrants in

Riverside and San Bernadino counties to sell for scrap metal, according to police. It's believed the thief posed as a repairman, unbolted the 80-100 pound hydrants, and hauled them away in broad daylight.

Times are hard all over folks...

Suffolk, VA: It is often said when you gotta go, you gotta go --even after committing a crime. A 43 year old man was charged with robbery in Suffolk after allegedly knocking off a convenience store. Police caught him minutes later -- urinating behind the store he had robbed, still with the stolen cash.

He must have been nervous -- couldn't hold it any longer...

Stevens Point, WI: Wisconsin police arrested a 41 year old woman who had hit four people in a vicious blow-dart spree. Paula Wolf allegedly was driving around Stevens Point in a van and blowing darts at pedestrians. When police stopped her they also found a slingshot and a bucket of rocks. Wolf said she did it because "she likes hearing people say 'ouch.' "

Senora es muy loco!

Maryland: A burglary suspect found dangling out a vent in a Maryland convenience store tried to explain how he got there by telling police it was a game of hide and seek that had gone terribly wrong. He claimed that when his pals couldn't find him they fled, leaving him to face police.

Plausible deniability without the "plausible" part, maybe?

Michigan: The only mind altering substance was catnip. A Michigan hazmat team was called in after a landlord said she thought a tenant was making crystal meth because of the strong chemical smell only to discover the house was filled with cats. The litter boxes filled the house with the stench of ammonia, a key ingredient in meth.

Nothing worse smelling than a lot of cat pee --PHEW!

California: Talk about stupid! A California man was arrested after burning down his mobile home while cleaning his bong with rubbing alcohol. After Andrew Garcia spilled some of the alcohol on the ground, he lit it on fire in an effort to clean up, but accidentally ignited the drapes.

Si, El Stupido...

Maine: Two men were arrested for four burglaries in Maine after police placed them in the targeted homes with the help of the electronic monitoring bracelets they were wearing for earlier crimes.

They may as well have held up a sign! Crooks can be so stupid.

Iowa: Here we have a one stop shopping place for committing sin and then confessing. A thief broke into an Iowa church just to use its TV and DVD player to watch pornography. When church officials came in the following day, they found the man had cooked himself a meal and fallen asleep in front of a TV blaring sex videos.

Naughty boy.

Detroit, MI: An anti-prostitution activist is on the hook after finding himself on the wrong side of the law. The 51-year old Detroit man was arrested for impersonating an officer, flashing a badge at a streetwalker and yelling, "Get off the Street!" The woman turned out to be an undercover female officer -- although she was out to bag johns, not loudmouths.

Hoist by his own petard!

Los Angeles, CA: Which side of the screen was the horror on? A theatergoer at an LA screening of the movie "Shutter Island" was stabbed in the neck with a meat thermometer after he tried to hush another man who was talking loudly on his cell phone. Police said, "It was a vicious and cowardly attack."

...and that the movie stunk!

Austin, TX: Police in Texas said they arrested a former auto dealership worker who allegedly used a computer to disable more than 100 vehicles after he was fired. Austin police said Omar Ramos-Lopez, 20, who was fired from his position as a collector for Texas Auto Center in January, used his home computer on March 2nd to access the dealership's Web site and disable the engines and activate the horns of more than 100 vehicles sold by the business, the Austin American-Statesman reported. "He was the collector for Texas Auto Center, so he had the password and all the necessary requirements to get into the system and manipulate the vehicles," Sgt. Keith Bazzle said. The system is in place so the dealership can deactivate vehicles when customers fail to make payments, company officials said. They said further security measures are being implemented to prevent similar incidents in the future. Ramos-Lopez was arrested Wednesday after police traced his computer's IP address. He was charged with felony breach of computer security and jailed in lieu of $3,000 bail.

Idiot!

Springfield, MA: Massachusetts police are hunting for two men who robbed a woman after she walked into a pub and flashed $27,000 in cash. The woman bragged about getting the money in an insurance payout. The men waited for her outside the bar with a gun.

Heard the one about the idiot with money who walks into a bar.....

Indianapolis, IN: An armed robber walked into an Indianapolis check-cashing store and, when the clerk started crying and talking about God, the gun-toting thief prayed with her. Then he walked off with $20 -- before his guilty conscience made him turn himself in the next day.

Thank you Jesus, thank you Lord. The sinner is saved.

Duluth, MN: This one is not about robbery. This one is about a guy who had his beer and drank it, too. Dennis LeRoy Anderson was charged with DWI after crashing his motorized La-Z-boy lounger into a parked car as he motored away from his local bar in Duluth. Anderson, 62, who had had nine beers before hopping into the contraption, claimed he was driving fine until a woman jumped in front of him, knocking him off course.

Cherche La Femme, as the French would say.

Louisiana: He was breaking up with her, but still... A Louisiana woman was arrested for cooking her man a hot breakfast -- and dumping it on him. Carolyn Brown, 44, allegedly dumped scalding hot grits over her boyfriend after he announced he was leaving her. He was treated for second-degree burns, and she was arrested by police.

YOW!!

Washington, DC: A dumb amateur chef was arrested for whipping up a batch of chicken a la cocaine. The Guatemalan gourmand was nabbed at Washington's Dulles Airport trying to smuggle in a fully cooked chicken stuffed with $4,000 worth of the white powder narcotic.

I like it -- chicken a la cocaine. Is that anything like coq au vin?

England: Meanwhile, speaking of poultry, here's a fowl fetish. A deranged man in England was accused of being a chicken licker. Adeel Ayub, 20, was charged with criminal damage after supermarket surveillance video caught him licking raw chickens and putting them back on the rack. He also smashed eggs and slashed customers' garments.

Deranged, indeed... Chicken licking, ugh.

Charlotte, NC: North Carolina Alcohol Enforcement Agents busted a woman for allegedly selling moonshine out of her day-care center in Charlotte. There were kids inside the center when an undercover agent went in to buy two gallons of the rot gut, authorities said. The woman claimed she was holding a package for someone and had no clue what was in it.

Boy, haven't we heard that tale before!

Dallas, TX: Police in Dallas are under fire for giving tickets to drivers who do not speak English. The rogue language enforcers were slapping violators with $204 fines, even though there is no law saying drivers must speak English. Police Chief David Kunkle said he will cancel the fines.

Que estupido!

Bedford. VA: The headline read: "Cops got woman's goat – literally." When police stopped the 32-year-old motorist at a DUI checkpoint in Bedford they heard a kicking noise coming from the back. It turned out to be a goat, bound and shoved into the trunk, where it was 94 degrees. Police removed the goat and charged the woman with cruelty to animals. The goat was given water and taken to an animal shelter.

Baaaaaaa.....

Rapid City, SD: This is about one honest thief. Lonnie Pannell, of Rapid City, robbed a bank and got away with $2,800, police said. He was arrested about a day later. When he was booked into jail, an officer filling out a form asked him for his occupation. "Robbery," he replied.

Ol' honest Abe...

Weymouth, MA: Massachusetts police were on poop patrol after they got a search warrant to inspect the bowel movements of a suspect who had allegedly swallowed a huge stash of drugs. After the suspect was taken to the hospital, Weymouth police combed through his fecal matter and found seven bags of heroin, eleven bags of cocaine and two bags of crack.

Phew! What a load.

Pine Lawn, MO: Police in Pine Lawn arrested an angry woman after she allegedly shot at her husband when he refused to give her some of their tax-return money. Thankfully, she missed. Assistant Police Chief Daniel O'Conner said the woman felt "more than justified" about the shooting. Nevertheless, she's been charged with first degree assault.

What is mine is mine and what is yours is mine....

Gilbert, AZ: We have all heard of the cases where pot smokers call 911 to report their marijuana stolen. This one provides a new twist. An Arizona man was arrested after he put up his marijuana stash up for sale of Graigslist. The silly guy from Arizona offered to trade his weed and an iPod for an iPad.

Technology surely got him in trouble...police do read Craigslist!

Alexandria, LA: A jail trustee in Louisiana assigned to work outside the prison walls smuggled cigarettes, loose tobacco and prescription pills into the prison for other inmates – stashing the contraband inside his prosthetic leg.

Bet they don't trustee him now!

Los Angeles, CA: Sony Dong, 46, who smuggled 14 Asian songbirds into LA by hiding them under his pants legs during a flight from Vietnam, has been sentenced to four months in jail. Dong, who had pleaded guilty to illegally importing wildlife, also has to pay $4,000 toward the care of the birds.

What a sad song! We wonder how he kept the songbirds quiet during the long flight from Vietnam??

Spokane, WA: Recently police in Spokane found $26,000 hidden in a Ms. Harris' very ample bra after she had been arrested in connection with an alleged fraud ring that authorities said used fake driver's licenses and counterfeit credit cards. As the 6 foot,

400 pound Harris was being booked, jail guards found the cash and bank receipts stashed in her bra.

She's a big girl but she's not fat, she's just big-boned....

WISCONSIN: A Wisconsin woman kept a non-working freezer filled with 100 dead cats at her home. Gabriella Bernabei said she is a Wiccan and has been collecting the cats with the intention of "returning them to Mother Earth" when the time is right. The police were not sympathetic and seized the cat carcasses — Bernabei is contemplating suing the police for a violation of her religious freedom.

Good luck with that suit! 100 dead cats, yuck!

Pittsburgh, PA: Police are on the lookout for a "butter-fingered" bandit who robbed a convenience store of $66, then dropped all but $1 as he fled the scene. The gun toting thief, wearing a ski mask did manage to also make off with seven packs of cigarettes during the silly heist.

At today's prices seven packs of smokes cost almost $40 bucks.

CHAPTER TWO

Weird criminal law stories from the state of Florida.

Professor Birdsong lives in Florida. It is a wonderful state. But the state produces lots of weird criminal law stories. They are all true. Here are a few from 2010.

New Port Richey: A 32-year-old Newport Richey man who called 911 to complain about his mother is facing criminal charges. According to the Pasco County Sheriff's Department, Charles Dennison told a deputy that his mother took his beer during a Memorial Day, 2010, cookout and he wanted her arrested. Dennison told the deputy that he would continue to call 911 if his mother wasn't arrested. Dennison was charged with making false 911 calls and jailed on $150 bond. The deputy stated that Dennison appeared "very intoxicated" when the deputy had arrived at the man's home.

Yep, cherche la booze....

Florida: Here is a real ass! A Florida man who was charged with flashing a mother and daughter in a parking lot said that it was all a misunderstanding and that he dropped his pants only because he had "explosive diarrhea." Unfortunately, the police investigator who checked David Napodano's "tighty whities," found no evidence to support his story, so he was charged with indecent exposure.

What an ass.

Florida: The headline read: "Even rock stars aren't this dumb about partying." A Florida man died in the Spring of 2010, of a drug overdose after celebrating passing his court ordered drug test by going out on a massive morphine binge. After Michael Berg, 23, had been out drinking vodka and beer with friends he decided to drink a shot glass full of morphine and was found dead several hours later.

How foolish. How sad...OD City!

Naples: They call it the tune-up to the tune of $50,000. A Naples auto mechanic who took a client's 2008 Porsche for a "diagnostics" test run flipped the car at 164 mph as he took it around a curve. Kenneth Kasten, 50, walked away without a scratch, the Florida Highway Patrol reported. But, he was charged with reckless driving and leaving the scene of a crash, and he has to make good on the damages. Kasten got one break -- he was not charged with theft, since the owner technically gave him the car when she dropped it off for service.

ZOOM! CRASH! BOOM!

Marion County: Florida students whose lockers were frequently getting broken into used a cell phone camera to catch the culprit -- their gym teacher. Deputies from the County Sheriff's office arrested teacher Steven Simmons after students showed them images of him stealing cash from their lockers. The North Marion High School teacher later confessed that he had stolen $400.

Bad teacher! Baaaad teacher! Gimme 100 pushups and jail time...

Florida: A Florida motorist ran a red light on US Highway 98 even though a deputy sheriff's car was right behind him. Then he made a left turn, stopped his vehicle and tried to hide in the back seat. Police who arrested Charles Jesse Johnson, 40, found he had seven license suspensions and four revocations on his record.

He just can't catch a break!

Brevard County: Commissioners in Brevard unanimously passed a bill exempting horse owners from a pooper-scooper law. Horse owner Wanette Dyer testified, "To stop a 1,000-pound animal, get off, hold it while you try to put the poop in a bag is just not a good idea."

The newspaper headline read: "Only a horse's ass would have voted "neigh."

Orange County: It was the case of Mickey Mouse v. Donald Duck. The famed mouse has filed a trademark infringement case against his duck pal in Orange County court. The filing is more than likely the work of a prankster. Why? Well, Mickey Mouse is being represented by Juan Abogado of Candy Cane Lane. Donald Duck is being represented by Pluto.

As you probably know -- Abogado-- means lawyer in Spanish.

Florida: Oops! Parents of uninsured Florida children called the governor's office for help and were directed to dial the toll free number of the state's KidCare line. But two numbers were transposed -- and they got a sex line instead. Callers were greeted with, "Hey there, sexy guy," and offered a more graphic conversation for $2.99 a minute.

Some KidCare, I'd say...

Florida: He became a real meathead! Elsie Egan, 53, was arrested by Dunnellon police after she repeatedly slapped her live-in boyfriend in the face with a raw steak, all because he refused a slice of bread and asked for a roll. Egan was charged with abuse.

Temper... Temper...

Florida: This one is about a mystery that was too realistic and tragic. A Florida murder-thriller dinner train was halted after fatally striking a man lying on the tracks. Police believe the victim had fallen asleep. The train riders had paid $75 for a scenic train ride, five course meal and some dinner theater.

How does one happen to fall asleep on railway tracks?

Florida: This Florida man was so anxious to go to prison, he told 911 that he had killed his wife. When police showed up at Ronald Conkright's St. Petersburg home, he couldn't produce a body and admitted he was single. He then showed them 20 grams of marijuana on a table. "You can arrest me now," he said. They did.

Idiot. Most people want to stay out of prison.

Florida: Claudia De La Rosa is the kind of team player any company would want. The Florida secretary was arrested after allegedly calling in a bomb threat to the Miami International Airport -- just so her late running boss wouldn't miss his flight.

Misplaced loyalty...

Tampa: A man who posed as his identical twin brother at a Florida hearing was found in contempt of court after a lawyer picked up on the switch. Marcus Mauceri said he did it because his brother, Matthew, was unable to make it to court on time for the opening of his fraud case. Marcus got 179 days in jail.

How ironic -- a switcheroo at a fraud trial.

Tampa: An angry mother is suing a Tampa strip club, for hiring her 16 year old daughter as a nude dancer. Valorie Duran alleges in her suit that the Emperors Gentleman's Club should have done their homework and checked on her birth date before hiring her. It appears that the daughter ran away several months ago and sought employment at the club.

Careful! Sixteen may get you 20...

Orlando: And it is not yet summer! It has been reported that "cold-blooded thieves" in Orlando have made off with at least 95 air conditioners in the first four months of 2010. It is further reported that this was nearly double the rate of all the A/C thefts from 2009.

Brrrrrrr.......

Palm, Harbor: Palm Harbor police officer, Richard Nalven, wrestled an 8 foot alligator after it turned up at a busy intersection. Nalven then used his handcuffs to immobilize the gator's rear legs.

Only in Florida...

Putnam County: A sheriff's deputy arrested a beekeeper for allegedly taking bees, honey and equipment from beekeeping rivals. Police contend they found Ruben Josey, 45, in possession of 48 stolen hives and other goods worth thousands of dollars.

The headline read: "It's a stinging indictment." Yuk, yuk, yuk...

Jacksonville: A homeless man walked into a Jacksonville pet store and stole a live ferret by stuffing it in his pants. When a teenager approached Rodney Bolton in the parking lot, the thief tossed the ferret in the young man's face, leaving scratches and bite marks, police said. Bolton was charged with battery with a "special weapon."

Colloquy at the jail: Q. Hey man, what are you in for? A. Assault with a Deadly Ferret!

Bradenton: A Bradenton man was arrested after calling 911 operators 18 times in two months. David Bouchard, 55, called about non-emergency situations, and he wound up in handcuffs after phoning in claiming a cop was kissing a prostitute near his home. Trouble was, the cop was at the woman's home only because Bouchard had called 911 a few minutes before because he "had a feeling" something was wrong.

What was wrong is that Bouchard is a troubled, lonely idiot.

Florida: It was a quick heist done in by "quick sand." A Florida man was arrested for stealing sand from a public beach after loading so much into his Ford F-150 that the wheels sunk into the ground, halting his getaway. Police soon arrived and discovered Brian Splain, 46, standing next to a hole in the beach. He was dead drunk!

Naturally...

Florida: This one sure saved everyone a lot of time. Three women were arrested after showing up for a Florida drug hearing with drugs on them. Among them, they had dozens of pills and a syringe, as well as a tourniquet. All three were there to give urine samples to prove they were keeping up with their ordered drug treatment.

How stupid!

Weird Criminal Law Stories

Florida does produce an abundance of weird criminal law stories. Here are a few more for your consideration from 2009.

Lake Mary: A 35-year-old Kristie Lee Mathis was arrested and faces 12 counts of unlawful sexual activity with a minor. This after the parents of a 17-year-old complained to the police about her involvement with their son. The teenager told police that between mid May and mid July there were at least 12 incidents of sexual activity between him and Mathis. Police arrested Mathis at a Bar near Lake Mary a short time after she drove away from a traffic stop in which she had been a passenger in a vehicle driven by the 17 year old victim. Her bail was set at $12,000.

PYT. Seems she likes pretty young things.

Sanford: A few days later this story appeared in the Orlando area news: Kristie Lee Mathis, a 35 year old Lake Mary woman, already facing charges of sexual activity with a 17 year old boy just days before was charged with lewd and lascivious behavior involving a 14 year old boy as she was being released from jail on bond. The new charge stems from an allegation by the boy who told police that in March he was at the woman's home and they were sitting on her couch watching a movie when she began to rub him through his clothes. The boy said he grabbed her hand and made her stop.

Good for him!

Tallahassee: It's a crime against humanity to wear nothing but a banana hammock while riding on a banana seat in Florida. A 55 year old man known for riding a bike around Tallahassee wearing just a thong, and therefore frequently exposing himself, has been arrested. Richard Irby is notorious for walking around his trailer park with his genitals hanging from his skivvies.

Ewwwww...What a perv.

Ft. Lauderdale: A former Florida city commissioner who had launched a program to combat bike theft had his own ride stolen. Tim Smith of Ft. Lauderdale, noticed a traffic accident as he cycled near a beach and went to help. When He returned for his bike, it was gone. To make matters worse, Smith failed to follow his own campaign's advice, and had to admit to cops that he had not registered his own bike!

Sounds like the very definition of "ironic."

Fort Walton Beach: A 34 year old wife was arrested in Florida for allegedly assaulting her husband after spotting him licking another woman's face. She dragged him out of a bar in Fort Walton Beach -- by his hair -- while hitting him.

Where is a rolling pin when a lady needs one?

Tampa: A Tampa man triggered a manhunt after he lied to his wife about being kidnapped so he could be with his girlfriend, police said. Wikler Moran-Mora sent his wife a text telling her he had been abducted and was being held for ransom.

CHEATER!

Brevard County: Sylvester Jiles, who had been released days earlier from the Brevard County jail, decided he would be much safer inside after his life was threatened by people outside. So he tried to get back in by jumping the prison fence -- and fell through three levels of barbed wire. He was taken to a hospital. This is how his fall may have sounded:

OUCH! OUCH! YOW! DAMN! LORDY! OW! OW! WHUMP.....

Florida: A 92-year old man plowed his car through the front window of a Florida restaurant and then walked inside and ordered breakfast. Neither the man nor any of the customers at "Biscuits 'N' Gravy & More" were hurt.

He was obviously in a hurry for the early bird special.

Fort Lauderdale: Police in Fort Lauderdale sent letters to known fugitives promising them a "stimulus check" from the government. The suspects were asked to call a hotline and set up an appointment to pick up a check from an auditorium where "South Florida Stimulus Coalition" banners hung. When the fugitives arrived, they were identified and about 75 were arrested on offenses ranging from grand theft to fraud to attempted murder. Police say that the two day sting was dubbed "Operation Show Me The Money."

That's why we call it FloriDUH!

Sarasota: Florida scientists are trying to track down an underwater robot nicknamed "Waldo" that mysteriously vanished in the waters of the Gulf Coast. The remote controlled, $100,000 robot equipped with a detector to find red tide, a toxic algae bloom, has been missing for a week from the Mote Marine laboratory in Sarasota.

Where's Waldo????

Pensacola: A burglar who made off with a Pensacola man's valuables returned to the home later and snatched what he could not carry on his first trip -- a 100 pound plasma screen TV. The kicker to the story -- a police officer was on the scene investigating the first burglary when the thief made off with the TV. The owner of the house said the thief had already stolen his wallet, watch and video game system. Investigators had left the TV in the backyard, where the burglar put it, so they could dust for fingerprints. Police have offered to pay for the TV.

Gutsy burglar!

Fort Pierce: A woman broke into a car parked at a Fort Pierce police station to get change for the soda machine. Sophia Paulinyce, 19, was arrested for stealing $7 from a police officer's private vehicle and charged with felony burglary and misdemeanor larceny. Paulinyce apologized to the officers for her illegal and dumb bid to quench her thirst.

Next time just use the water fountain Paulinyce.......

Jensen Beach: This Florida man has been accused of downloading 1,000 images of child pornography. He blames his cat! Keith Griffin of Jensen Beach told investigators that his cat jumped on the computer keyboard while he was downloading music. It was all a mistake.

Right, a mistake that the cat repeated 1,000 times!

Orlando: A 60 year old man was convicted in August, 2009, of groping Minnie Mouse at Disney World. William Moyer of Cressona PA., claimed he was innocent of sexually assaulting the costumed park employee. But the victim testified in court that "she had to do everything possible to keep Moyer's hands off her breasts. Moyer was found guilty of misdemeanor battery. He must write the victim a letter of apology, serve 180 days probation, complete 50 hours of community service, pay $1,000 in court costs and undergo a mental evaluation.

Call him a "Minnie perv."

Tampa: Inmates at a Tampa jail are really feeling the heat. Prisoners at the minimum security lockup are selling bottles of hot sauce made from peppers grown at the jail. The $7 bottles are labeled "No Escape," among other things. The inmates have made $10,000 on the sauce, proceeds of which are used to keep up the greenhouse and to buy basic supplies.

The crime here is charging $7 for a bottle of hot sauce!

Tampa: A Tampa doctor was given two years probation after admitting he removed a bullet from a fugitive shot by U.S. Marshals, hid the slug, and lied to investigators about it. Dr. David Ciesla got caught when a med student saw him slip the slug into his surgical glove.

Snitch!

Ft. Pierce, FL: A Florida man accused of killing his son-in-law in New Jersey is arguing that he was unable to commit the crime because he was too fat. When Edward Ates took the witness stand in his own defense he told jurors he would not have had the energy to climb and descend the staircase where prosecutors say the killer was perched when he shot Paul Duncsak, a 40-year-old pharmaceutical executive, in 2006. An attorney for Ates claims that in 2006, the 62 year old who stood 5 feet 8 inches and tipped the scales at 285 pounds, was in such bad physical shape that he could not have pulled off the shooting or the fast getaway the killer made.

Good argument. However, the jury didn't buy it. Guilty!

Naples, FL: A Florida fortune teller is being sued for failing to pay back a "spiritual loan" of $13,200. Eumathe Dufrene, 53, said she loaned the seer the cash with the promise it would be returned once the evil hanging over her family was lifted. Now it's up to a judge in Naples to determine whether or not the fortune teller, Dorothy Johnson, succeeded.

Yeah, right! Good luck with that one.

Miami: A defense attorney claims she was not allowed to visit her client at a federal detention center in Miami because of her bra. It appears that her underwire bra set off the metal detector, and guards would not let her inside. After removing her bra in the women's room, the attorney was still refused entrance by the guards because she wasn't wearing a bra.

Talk about a catch-22!

Volusia County, FL: Some people do not like being the butt of a practical joke! The Daytona Beach News-Journal reported in February 2010, that a Volusia County man had his pants pulled down by his roommate as he climbed a ladder, so he responded by pulling a gun and knife on his pants pulling roommate. The prankster suffered cuts to his hand during the confrontation that followed -- and also had the barrel of a 12-gauge shotgun pressed against the back of his head. After being released from the hospital, he trashed their house with barbecue sauce, fruit juice, cooking oil, mustard, gasoline and a fire extinguisher. Police are looking for him.

The headline read: "Volusia man gets pantsed, grabs shotgun and goes after prankster." Good headline, but it just doesn't tell the whole story.

CHAPTER THREE

Weird criminal law stories from Germany.

Years ago Professor Birdsong was stationed in Germany as a U.S. State Department officer. He had a great time living in Hamburg. He has kept up with events in Germany ever since. Here are a few weird criminal law stories from Germany from 2009 and 2010. Enjoy. Ja voll!

Germany: A German drunkard stumbled into an open drain and got stuck in the hole because of his beer gut. Gerhard Wilder, 46, was so tightly wedged in, police called firefighters to free him. He has vowed to go on a diet and cut back on his beer intake after embarrassing photos of him showed up on the Internet.

Sounds like he was a whopper.

GERMANY: A German woman called police after hearing someone climbing up her balcony. Police found it was just her boyfriend bringing flowers and a bottle of wine, but they still arrested him on an outstanding warrant. "He was trying to be romantic, but it all went wrong," said a police spokesperson.

Next time, just send flowers Dumkopf!

GERMANY: The world's biggest underwear thief is now locked up. German police uncovered 1,000 pair of underpants after they caught a 46-year old man swiping three more. He claimed he acquired them in car-trunk sales and over the Internet.

There is a whole lot more to this story that Birdsong just does not want to know...

GERMANY: A 66-year-old man started trouble with his 63-year-old next door neighbor in a fight over a strip of lawn between their two properties. The older man poured a bucket of water over his neighbor's head for making too much noise while he was trimming the grassy strip. The soaked 63-year-old then attacked his older rival with a weed whacker. He was charged with attempted murder.

This silly one will surely end in a plea to something lesser than attempted murder!

GERMANY: This really isn't a crime but it seems criminal. The German newspaper, *Bild Zeitung*, reported in May 2010, that a

German mailman married his cat in an elaborate ceremony. Uwe Mitzscherlich, 39, told the newspaper he wanted to marry his 15-year-old, obese, asthmatic feline, Cecilia, before she died. "We cuddle all the time, and she has always slept in my bed," said Ewe. The *Bild* further reports that the groom was dressed in a top hat and tails and the bride wore a white dress and meowed throughout the ceremony.

Like I said, maybe not a crime but it seems criminal... This one turns same sex marriage on its head!

GERMANY: A German bank robber is upset that his cat cannot visit him in jail -- because he says the kitty is a reincarnation of his dead mother. Peter Koenig, a Buddhist, told a judge: "I know it's Mommy. She looks after me just the way she did. I need to see her the way other prisoners see their wives and children." The judge barred a visit, but allowed him to write to the cat.

That judge is a real comedian...

GERMANY: A German crook decided to quit while he was still behind. The 24-year old tried to rob two hotels -- and in each case fled empty handed with security guards chasing him. Then he tried but failed to break into the local tax office in Muelheim an der Ruhr. Finally, the bandit wannabe gave up without a fuss after being trapped in a getaway van he used to ram an armored car. "He needs a change of job," said one police officer.

Sounds like he will get a new one in jail!

GERMANY: A robbery gang in Malliss detonated a hugely powerful explosive device in an attempt to blast open a bank's ATM machine. The explosion practically destroyed the building -- but the ATM survived intact. It is further reported that the embarrassed thieves fled empty handed.

KA-BOOM

GERMANY: German police billed a 19 year old reptile lover $135,000 to pay for the massive emergency response required when his poisonous pet cobra escaped. It took three weeks of pulling up floorboards and evacuating apartments in the man's building before they found the slitherer -- who had died.

What a bad investment!

Germany: A jealous husband in Germany hired assassins who four times botched hit jobs on his wife. The first attempt failed when the target never showed; the second when a group of school children disrupted the killer; a third came when a neighbor sauntered by; and finally when the woman managed to escape the attack.

Hit and miss assassins... It's cheaper to keep her.

GERMANY: How awkward could this have been! A woman in Germany called police after hearing strange sounds coming from her bedroom, only to turn beet red when officers discovered that her vibrator had accidentally turned on in a drawer. "The tenant's face abruptly changed color," a police spokesman said. "The officers wished her a nice evening and left."

BZZZZZZZZZZZZ....

Germany: It is unlawful in Germany to manufacture, possess or display any objects glorifying the Third Reich. Recently, German prosecutors have been investigating an artist who created a series of garden gnomes with their arms raised in a Nazi salute. Investigators, however, are not sure if the artist is pro-Hitler or just ridiculing the Third Reich. "It will depend on what the artist and the owners of the gallery have to say for themselves," said a prosecution spokesman.

SIEG HEIL!

GERMANY: It is reported in July 2009, that a car thief stole the limo of Germany's health minister while she was on vacation in Spain.

Someone broke into the room of Health Minister Ulla Schmidt's chauffer, grabbed the car keys and made off with the black Mercedes, said a Health Ministry spokesperson.

GESUNDHIET!

GERMANY: A German potato farmer got a ticket in the mail claiming a speed camera clocked him going 76 mph on his tractor, along with a picture of him going through the speed trap. "My tractor is fairly modern and got a good motor, but I can guarantee it is no supercar." Thorsten Holck said.

If there was such a tractor, potato farming would be more fun....

GERMANY: A blitzed Berlin bride spent her wedding night passed out next to a crate of vodka in the back seat of a BMW. Police in Cologne said the inebriated 30 year old, still clad in her wedding dress, remained unconscious even after rescuers smashed the window to free her from the car.

BETRUNKEN! GOTT IN HIMMEL... VAROOM?

GERMANY: This one is about one last hurrah before going up the river. A 41-year old German man called in by police for questioning about a robbery popped in and robbed another shop on his way to the police station. When he arrived, police noticed he bore a striking resemblance to the description the shopkeeper had just called in. Plus, he had the stolen loot in his car.

What a numbskull!

GERMANY: A man who stole a van outside a German circus was so terrified when he realized there was a lion in the back that he crashed into a wall. The thief apparently noticed what his cargo was only when the big cat let out a bone-chilling roar. The cat was fine. The thief got away. No arrest was made.

The King of the Jungle wins again.

GERMANY: Nope! It was not armed robbery. A man with no arms managed to steal a TV from a German store. He made off with the 24-inch set using clamps that had been attached to his body by an accomplice. "It's hard to believe that the sight of an armless man walking along with TV clamped to his body did not get anyone's attention," a police officer remarked.

Hands up! Ooopps...sorry....

GERMANY: Everyone would have been better off if this fellow had just ordered decaf. A German man walked into an arcade and ordered a cup of coffee and then threatened to break the mug over the cashier's head if she didn't hand over the money from the register.

Bad customer!

GERMANY: A German robber knocked over a bank branch twice in 24 hours, just a week after he had been released from prison -- for robbing the same branch. He even reminded the tellers who he was, shouting, "I was here

yesterday, and I want money again today!"
He made off with $600 but was picked up
three hours later.

Yep, old habits die hard....

Weird Criminal Law Stories

CHAPTER FOUR

Weird Criminal Law Stories from the rest of Europe and the World from 2009 and 2010.

New Zealand: She was a real boob! A New Zealand teenager who was flashing her breasts at passing drivers was run over by a motorist who was so distracted by the site that he ran off the road. Cherelle May Dudfield, 18, was only slightly hurt and was charged with disorderly conduct for the drunken stunt.

Yep, we thought alcohol might have been involved...

UNITED KINGDOM: Freedom of speech has its limits! A British woman lost her appeal against a court ordered ban of her deafeningly loud sex sessions, which led neighbors to call police -- thinking someone was being killed. Caroline Cartwright, 48, said it was a violation of her human rights, but a judge said it was actually just a "nuisance."

Shhhhhhhhhhhhhhhhhh...!

Sweden: These folks certainly were not trying to keep their romance secret. A Swedish couple made so much noise in bed that their landlord tried to evict them. "Their screams of passion were so loud, I could hear them three floors away," said one building resident. "I don't think they were playing cards."

Betcha they were faking it...

SCOTLAND: This 22-year-old woman in Scotland really loved her handbag. She held on so tightly when a man in a car tried to snatch away her Louis Vuitton that she was dragged down the street alongside the moving vehicle until he finally let go. The woman was hospitalized with cuts and bruises, but still has her Vuitton bag.

Sounds like the words to that old song: Hold tight, hold tight, hold tight, I want   some sea food mama...

SWITZERLAND: This one is about a driver who didn't do his bit for the environment. A Swiss driver accidentally hit the gas and plunged 30 feet into a giant recycling bin.

The man was only slightly hurt, but was given a $75 fine for mixing metals and plastics.

Shameful!

Siberia, RUSSIA: A 45-year old Siberian woman, who cannot stop killing her mates, was convicted of fatally stabbing her third lover and will now spend the next 12 years behind bars, according to authorities. Irina Rybalko previously convicted of killing her husband in 1992 and a boyfriend in 1997, was sent to a prison colony, a Novosibrisk legal department spokesman said.

Sounds like a "black widow." Men beware!

AUSTRALIA: An Australian woman woke up to find an intruder standing over her bed, with her bra on his head and a tub of ice cream and a can of tuna tucked under his arm. The 61-year-old woman then gave chase, hauling her catheter bag with her into the street, where the man was soon arrested.

Weird stuff... a bra, ice cream and tuna! Ice cream and tuna do not mix well.

MALAYSIA: Malaysian police arrested a Lebanese man with $66 million in counterfeit US currency after he left a $500 bill as a tip for hotel staff. Since the largest US note in circulation is a $100, staffers called police who found him in possession of phony $1 million, $100,000 and $500 bills.

It's all about the "Benjamins!"

SWEDEN: A Swedish man who claimed to be confined to a wheelchair was nabbed for swindling the government disability system after police found a photo of him dancing with a costumed rabbit mascot at an amusement park. His relatives were also charged because the swindler claimed they were helping care for him.

CROOK!

Mexico City, MEXIC0: Several Mexican laboratories are offering a special DNA testing package for people who think their significant other is cheating. "They can bring us underwear, a sheet, chewing gum, anything which will provide testers with traces of sperm, saliva, or hair," said the director of one lab. The process can cost up to $500.

Mexican "players" be careful -- you have been warned...

Maldegem, BELGIUM: A clerk in a shoe store in Maldegem called police to complain about a bizarre robbery. One shoe had been stolen. Police easily tracked down the suspect -- a one-legged amputee. An arrest was made.

There was no need for Sherlock Holmes on this one!

UNITED KINGDOM: How Ghoulish! A woman who lost her arm in a car crash in England was aghast to discover that her wedding ring was stolen off the severed limb after being brought to the hospital. Hospital staffers say that the arm was incinerated and that there was no sign of the ring. Police are investigating.

Investigating! Sure....

Limoges, FRANCE: This is one way to avoid an exam. A 29 year old medical student in Limoges stabbed himself twice in the stomach before a scheduled residency examination. He then claimed he had been assaulted. Of course, it didn't work. It was discovered that the student had a history of pulling stunts to avoid exams and later admitted the he had stabbed himself. He faces a possible jail term for up to six months.

YOUCH!!!

Palermo, ITALY: It seems a judge in Palermo thought he was being lenient by sentencing Santo Gambino to house arrest for illegally dumping construction waste. He was wrong! After a few days, 30 year old Gambino left home and begged for a jail sentence because he could not stand his wife's "nonstop nagging." The judge sent him back home, ordering him to "try to get along" with his wife.

Heaven was never like this!

FRANCE: It is reported that a 20 year old video game nut, Julien Barreaux, hunted down a rival gamer who beat his character in the online game Counter-Strike and tried to stab him to death --in real life. Barreaux narrowly missed his opponent's heart and is now undergoing psychiatric tests.

Sacre Bleu! it's only a game. Get a life Julien!

UNITED KINGDOM: A British warehouse worker is kicking up a stink after he got fired for farting too much. Daniel Cambridge said he was canned from a supermarket warehouse because of his farts, but he claims he can't help himself. "It is a side effect of the anti-depression tablets I'm taking," he said. Warehouse officials declined comment.

Of course, he is depressed because he farts so much.

ROMANIA: A head start on a life of crime! Police investigating a burglary in a kindergarten in Romania were surprised to find the mastermind was a 5 year old boy. Several rooms had been ransacked, but the tip-off was theft of the nursery's entire collection of toys. The kid told police he "missed the toys and couldn't wait until school starts again."

Bad kid

HOLLAND: The Dutch parliament has banned sex between humans and animals, cutting the world off from the biggest supplier of bestiality videos. Experts say the Netherlands may supply something like 80 percent of the world's bestiality porn. Prior to the newly signed 2010 ban, it had been legal to have sex with animals as long as the nonhuman was not injured in any way.

Depravity will need a new home! Yuck... sex with animals

HOLLAND: A gang of burglars broke into a Dutch prison and stole the televisions from inmates' cells. The thieves broke into the minimum security cells while the inmates were out on weekend furloughs. Officials are still not sure exactly how the burglars got in.

They say, Jailbirds of a feather flock together. Bet they had inside help!

INDIA: Police in one town in India were wondering why their station house smelled so bad for the past two years. They then learned the source of the smell. They were shocked to find a rotting corpse that had been on the roof all that time. Police had meant to send the body to the coroner, but accidentally put it on the roof and forgot about it.

This is worse than the Keystone cops! Who would store a corpse on a roof of a police Station?

PAPAU, INDONESIA: Officials in Indonesia have decreed that anyone who has ever had penis enlargement is banned from becoming a police officer. An Applicant will now be asked if "his vital organ has been enlarged," said Papua police chief Bekto Suprapto. Officials believe the larger size causes a "hindrance during training."

Sounds painful too...

AUSTRALIA: Commentators say, if only she had suffered from the munchies rather than road rage, this story would have had a happier ending. An Australian woman who was high on amphetamines, anti-depressants and marijuana and had consumed two bottles of wine, freaked out when a man threw cheese balls at her car -- and ran him over, killing him. "She clearly wanted to teach the young man a lesson," a judge said.

So sad. So dead.

RUSSIA: A Russian Businessman who set up a museum dedicated to Josef Stalin was found bludgeoned and electrocuted. The body of

Vasily Bukhtiyenko was found at a tennis court in Volgograd, the city formerly known as Stalingrad. Police say the motive for the murder was unclear, but there has been resistance efforts to rehabilitate Stalin's image in Russia,

Resistance to rehabilitation...you think?

NEW ZEALAND: The headline read: "Good parenting may come in all sizes, but triple D is not one of them." A New Zealand father was arrested after leaving his 1 year old baby unattended for hours in a car while he was in a nearby strip club. A passer-by called police after seeing the tot sleeping in the car at 3 am. The father was found inside ogling the ladies.

Baaaaad Daaaad!

ARGENTINA: Talk about pulling the wool over their eyes! Two Argentine convicts escaped prison by disguising themselves as sheep and slipping away with a flock. The two covered themselves with full sheepskin fleeces and fashioned realistic looking heads for their getaway.

Baa, baaa black sheep…

UGANDA: The headline read: "Maybe these are flying nuns." Police found a huge marijuana crop in the garden of a convent in Uganda. One of the nuns told authorities they grow it for their farm animals – because of its supposed healthful benefits.

JMJ! JMJ! JMJ!

SWEDEN: A Swedish couple was charged with sexual deviancy for allegedly having sex in the back of a passenger bus. Other riders were aghast at the alleged love making on the ride through southern Sweden. the amorous couple denies the titillating allegations. "She only stroked me on my stomach inside my shirt," the man told police.

They should've gotten a room...

SCOTLAND: He was no victim! A 91 year old retired Scottish police officer and World War II hero fought off a burglar who broke into his home and tried to steal money and his medals. "He gave me a black eye, so I gave him one back," said William Hook. He expects the bandit to go to jail, but noted, "I've come through worse things in my life. I had a rough time as a POW, but I survived."

BOOM BOOM POW!

AUSTRALIA: A man bought a pair of scissors at an Australian 7-Eleven, and then gave them to a friend who used them to hold up another 7-Eleven down the block. While awaiting trial, one of the men robbed yet another 7-Eleven, stealing a soda and kicking down the front door after the clerk locked him inside.

Sounds like non-stop thieving...

INDONESIA: Two food vendors in Indonesia were arrested recently after they were caught selling meatballs made from the flesh of endangered monkeys. They said they had been using the monkey meat for a popular soup dish because it was cheaper than beef or chicken.

You know what not to eat on your next trip to Indonesia...

SWEDEN: This is a strange one. A suicidal man in Sweden called a help line -- and was stunned when the clergyman he was talking to fell asleep and started snoring five minutes into the conversation. But his call produced the hopped for result. The 44 year old man got so angry at the pastor, he said it gave him a new will to live.

ZZZZZZZZZ.........ZZZZZ......ZZZZ....

SPAIN: Spanish customs officials seized more than $1.5 million worth of bogus cigarettes that had been filled with rabbit droppings rather than tobacco. "They stunk. The smell just as you would imagine burning poo to smell," an official said. Twelve smugglers were arrested unloading the "crap" from a boat from China.

Guess rabbit droppings are cheaper than tobacco!

UNITED KINGDOM: British police arrested a man wearing a Snoopy costume while he attempted to break into a prison to spring a relative. The cartoon beagle had a gun -- which turned out to be a water pistol -- when he and an un-costumed helper turned up at the prison at the Isle of Wight.

SQUIRT!

UNITED KINGDOM: An English mother was fined $125 for feeding some ducks but was told her toddler son could carry on tossing bread because he was too little to be prosecuted. Officials say as an adult she should have known better. Vanessa Kelly, 26, says she refuses to pay the fine.

What a quack...

SPAIN: It's called butt profiling! Spanish customs officers stopped a man coming through Barcelona's airport because he had an unusually large behind -- and found 14 pounds of cocaine strapped to his rear. When investigators got to the bottom of it, they found a pair of neoprene pants with pockets holding 160 packages of coke.

A new twist on "Junk in the Trunk".....

EGYPT: An Egyptian was arrested recently at the Cairo airport for trying to smuggle eight live foxes and 50 chameleons – all in one large suitcase. The man had hoped to sell the animals in Thailand and buy a computer.

You know those chameleons would have never made it to Thailand....

St. Petersburg, RUSSIA: Recently there was a newspaper article under the headline; "In Russia, even the thieves live like Czars." Allegedly, Russian armed robbers made off with a truck carrying 13 tons of red caviar from a road near St. Petersburg. The haul was worth about $500,000. Still, the gang missed its mark. Red caviar, which comes from salmon, is much cheaper than black sturgeon caviar.

Pity, 13 tons is a lot of fish eggs from any kind of fish.

CHAPTER FIVE

Weird Criminal Law Stories from Chicago

Chicago is the headquarters of the American Bar Association. Professor Birdsong sometimes travels to Chicago on American Bar Association business. Chicago certainly has its share of weird criminal law stories. Here are a few of them of which he is fond.

May, 2010: A Woman who wore a T-shirt that read, "I own the [female sex organ] so I make the rules" in an Illinois courtroom was arrested for contempt of court by an offended female judge. Jennifer LaPenta, 19, was in court to lend support to a friend, and said she had not realized what shirt she had put on that day. As for her contempt arrest, LaPenta said "All the officers thought it was hilarious. It was humiliating."

Jennifer -- it's best not to advertise this kind of thing! We know it's yours!

May, 2010: A Chicago woman is suing a hair salon because she was hurt falling through its window from the sidewalk -- while trying to kick her husband after they had a few drinks. Melanie Shaker contends in her court papers that the window should have been fortified since it is on a street "frequently travelled by intoxicated pedestrians."

Now that is Chutzpa.

Christmas week 2009: Three armed, masked men barged into a Chicago home a week after Christmas 2009, and forced 11 people to take off their pants. They then shot one of the victims in the leg. The robbers then fled with the pants and televisions. Police speculate that the pants were stolen in order to get the victims' wallets and to prevent them from chasing the robbers.

Someone should have called the "fashion police."

May 2010: He must have been hungry. A mugger took the breakfast from a disabled woman on the South Side of Chicago in early May. Charles Johnson, 35, grabbed a slice of pizza from the 21 year old victim afflicted with cerebral palsy. Johnson who has prior convictions for armed robbery, forgery and burglary also took the young woman's handbag. He was chased down by passersby and then arrested by police. He is being held on bail of $150,000, while awaiting trial.

He probably misses prison.

August, 2009: Police in Northwest Chicago arrested a man they say was throwing heavy rocks from his Oldsmobile at other moving cars during a three week period. Daniel M. Phelan, 27, was arrested August 3rd after at least 10 reports of rocks hitting cars on a stretch of road between Ella Road and Illinois Route 59, say detectives. Asked by police why he was driving around with a pile of rocks on his passenger seat, Phelan said he was geologist. He later confessed that he collected the rocks in a forest preserve and on his way home he sometimes threw them out the window. Phelan told police, "If he hit anyone it was an accident." He was charged with five counts of misdemeanor reckless conduct and five counts of felony criminal damage to property. Police speculated that Phelan might have "some internal anger issues.

YOU THINK!!

August 2009: A mother rushing her terminally ill toddler to a hospital ran a red light and crashed into another vehicle Saturday morning in the Hyde Park neighborhood. Authorities confirmed that her 2 year old boy was dead, although the crash was not believed to have caused his death. The boy was suffering from leukemia and was in hospice care the Cook County medical examiner's office said.

The postman always rings twice….

August, 2009: The man who knocked down popular WLS-Channel 7 news anchor Cheryl Burton and punched five others in a fist-throwing rampage was committed Friday to six years in a state mental health facility. In June a Cook County Judge found Gregory Perdue not guilty by reason of insanity of aggravated battery charges for the April, 2008 punching spree on downtown State Street. The 28 year old suffers from schizophrenia.

We wonder if Burton's news reporting was so bad that it set him off?

August, 2009: It is over between the Chicago based William Wrigley, Jr. Company and

R&B singer Chris Brown. A Wrigley spokeswoman confirmed Thursday that the chewing gum giant had severed its ties with Brown in the wake of his guilty pleas to one count of felony assault on his girlfriend Rihanna. Brown had been at the center of an elaborate music-centric marketing plan for Wrigley's gum. Brown composed and sang the song *Forever,* which included the lyric "double your pleasure, double your fun." That song was subsequently incorporated as a jingle in Double mint gum commercials. When news of Brown's assault first surfaced Wrigley immediately suspended the commercial campaign. With the guilty pleas Wrigley has dropped Brown.

Silly ass singer!

August, 2009: An 86 year old Chicago woman was arrested for the 61st time over last weekend – for shoplifting anti-wrinkle cream from a North Side grocery store, police report. Ella Orko's first arrest, for petit larceny came in 1956. Her latest crime came on Sunday at the Dominick's Finer Foods grocery. An employee saw her stuff $225 worth of items into her pants before trying to leave without paying. Orko was charged with felony shoplifting and a Cook County judge ordered that she be held on $10,000 bail. Police say she has at least 20 aliases. Out of her 61 arrests, police say 13 resulted in convictions

Just call her "Klepto" Granny...

August, 2009: A South Side man was accused of endangering thousands of lives by allegedly impersonating a Chicago Transit Authority (CTA) traffic controller and radioing bogus instructions to subway train operators. Marcel Carter, 20, faces up to 20 years in prison and a $250,000 fine for breaking a federal law forbidding interference with transportation operators, say federal prosecutors. On or about June 2, 2009, Carter stole a CTA Kenwood radio transmitter and over several weeks transmitted instructions to train operators to disregard stop signals. None of his orders were obeyed. Carter was arrested a few days before this report when he and his brother asked a CTA employee at a subway train station if there was a reward for a stolen radio.

Crazy Doofuss!

August, 2009: A Somali born cabdriver, Abdinasir Kahin, wrestled with a cross-dressing, chain wielding suspected pickpocket in a dress and put him in a bear hug until police arrested him. The thief in the dress had already escaped from police once the same night after allegedly helping to beat a man bloody. While police struggled with the man's alleged partner in theft, Kahin saw the make-up wearing cross dresser return to grab a big white purse he had dropped before running away. That is when Kahin got out of his taxi and wrestled with and held the cross-dresser until an officer arrived to handcuff the thief.

Sounds horrible...a cross-dressing, chain wielding pickpocket in a dress...What next, Chicago?

August, 2009: Prosecutors leveled additional charges Thursday against four Burr Oak Cemetery workers accused of illegally unearthing old burial plots to make room for new graves. Carolyn Towns, 49; Keith Nicks, 45; his brother Terrence Nicks, 39, and Maurice Dailey, 59, were originally charged with dismembering human bodies last month after authorities revealed the alleged grave selling scheme at the Cemetery where 1,200 bone fragments have since been found. Yet, now, in the formal indictment handed down by the Cook County Court, the four face two counts each of aggravated theft of $100,000 to $500,000, unlawful removal of gravestones, desecration of human remains, unlawful removal of deceased human beings from a burial ground and conspiracy to dismember human remains. The most serious felonies carry penalties of from six to 30 years in prison. Towns, who was the cemetery manager allegedly, masterminded the scheme, which prosecutors said began in 2003.

There should be a special place in hell for these four fools!

February 2009: This fellow wanted to get caught. A stupid bank robber in Chicago handed a teller a note – written on the back of his pay stub. The FBI was able to track him down easily when he left behind the note bearing his name and address. The dope faces 20 years in jail.

D'OH!!

CHAPTER SIX

A Few Weird Criminal Law Stories in Closing from 2008 and 2009.

Here are some of Professor Birdsong's favorite weird stories from 2009:

Valentine, NE: Police in Valentine have finally nabbed the "Butt Bandit," a 35 year old man they believe had left greasy – and graphic –imprints of his buttocks and groin on the windows of stores, churches and schools for the past year. "This isn't normal behavior for Valentine, Nebraska," said Cherry County Attorney Eric Scott.

OK. We now know who did it…When do we find out why? What message was the "Butt Bandit" sending? Inquiring minds want to know…

Atlanta, GA: Rico Todriquez Wright, a rap artist was sentenced to 20 years in prison after killing a man and then writing a rap song that detailed how he did it and calling the victim, Chad Blue, by name. "Chad Blue you know how I shoot," rapped Wright in the song. "And now, so does everyone else."

Note to murderers: If you kill someone do not, I repeat, do not write a song describing how you did it.

Kentucky: A Kentucky inmate who escaped from prison returned later that same day – and pleaded with guards to let him back in. Chad Troy, 21, told police his family urged him to surrender because they feared for his safety. He said he immediately regretted running out the open prison door during a work detail. "I'm sorry about what I did," he said.

Either Chad's life on the outside must really suck or he figured it was easier to have sex inside the joint.

Lynchburg, VA: Bernard Wood, 33, was convicted of burglary and grand larceny in Lynchburg after prosecutors linked him to the crime scene by a greasy fingerprint. Wood apparently ate some fried chicken during the break-in and left his prints on a juice bottle.

Yep! He's finger-licking guilty!

Newport Beach, CA: Looks like the economy is so bad that even thieves are flocking to religion. At least, sort of. Bandits stole a 5-foot bronze statue of the Virgin Mary from a Newport Beach church, apparently to sell it as scrap. The statute was worth an estimated $30,000.

There is no shame left in this world when thieves steal a statute of the Most Blessed Virgin to sell as scrap!

Akron, OH: The AP reported after the 2008 presidential election that "There appear to be blue states and then there are booze states." An election night party in Akron turned ugly after the promoters offered a free drink for every state Barack Obama won. Obama nabbed 28 states plus Washington, D.C. The staggeringly drunken crowd rioted – resulting in a bouncer being shot.

OMG...democracy at work...sometimes a dangerous thing!

Fairbanks, AK: A motorist in Fairbanks was so drunk that he claimed he had no idea he was driving a stolen car until he was pulled over. Charles Schultz, whose blood alcohol level was more than twice the legal limit, thought he was driving his Chevy Cavalier until a trooper informed him he was actually behind the wheel of a Ford Escort.

Sounds like Schultz probably had too much Schlitz.

Indiana: It appears that poor parenting and drunkenness are a family affair for this Indiana family. Police pulled over a mother driving drunk with her 1-year old in the car. When they called the boy's father to pick him up, he showed up drunk. When they moved on to the grandparents, they, too, arrived very drunk! Finally, the police drove the boy safely home.

What a family of losers…

Niagara Falls, NY: They say this was not holy. A man importing bottles labeled "holy water" from Canada at the Niagara Falls border crossing was arrested when a federal drug-sniffing dog got a whiff of the water. It turned out to be ketamine, an animal tranquilizer sometimes used as an illegal party drug.

Holy cow!

England: An Englishman has been charged with animal cruelty for forcing a chicken to drink whisky and then blowing pot smoke in its face. The hen's owner called police and

Gary Maxwell, 21, was arrested. A judge called the episode a "horrible crime."

How "fowl!" Those English judges are given to overstatement at times…this is one of them.

Alaska: They have labeled him Gramps the Pusher. Police in Alaska arrested an 81-year old man for selling pain pills from his home. Police took 80 pills of OxyContin from Rayfield Dupree when he was arrested. He was charged with felony drug misconduct.

Who can live on social security alone, I ask you?

Spokane, WA: A 67 year old man, John Paul Adams allegedly walked into a gas station with a loaded .22 caliber rifle, told the clerk, "Give me what you got," and then ordered him to call the police after grabbing hundreds of dollars from the cash drawer. Adams went outside, unloaded his rifle, leaned it against the phone booth, and "stood there and waited for us," said Officer Tim Moses.

It's hard out there for a thief…prison is a much easier life.

Cincinnati, OH: Criminals – you are supposed to dispose of evidence – not create evidence! Police in Cincinnati were easily able to track down a man who stole a deaf woman's telephone after he snapped pictures of himself with the phone's camera. When the woman got a new phone and downloaded the snapshots from her account there was her thief staring right at her.

A dumb criminal for sure, but we are is still stuck on why a deaf woman has a cell phone....

Minnesota: A couple in this state was stunned to find a bag of crystal meth and $85 in their 7-year-old son's trick or treat bag. Police say the bag had a street value of $200. Apparently, an older kid had run by the couple's son and his sister and dropped the dope in the boy's bag.

The lesson for parents is always check that trick or treat bag when the little ones return home.

Benton, IL: Wonder if these cops got paid chicken feed. Police in Benton arrested an aggressive rooster that confronted a woman and a child. Officers detained the cock after what Chief, Mike O'Neill described as a brief scuffle. No one was injured, and the rooster was thrown into jail until its owner came to bail it out.

Now, that was one tough rooster!

Boise, ID: An Idaho man was charged with stealing $1,000 worth of cold cuts from a Boise grocery store. Police say the ham-handed man went to an Albertson's loaded up a cart with packaged meats, and wandered out without paying.

Sounds like one hungry thief.

Montague County, TX: Texas jailers shut down a jail facility that had turned into a basement lounge – with recliners in several cells and some prisoners having private locks on the doors of their home away from home. Others wrapped extension cords around bars as a means of keeping jailers out. The Texas Rangers finally put the clamps on the Montague County Jail, about 65 miles northwest of Fort Worth, and the inmates were shipped to nearby lockups.

Hey! Where do you think you are –home?

Portsmouth, NH: An elderly driver took getting lost to a whole new level when she took a few wrong turns and ended up cruising along an airport runway in New Hampshire. The unidentified, 70-year old motorist finally realized where she was and called police in terror because she thought she saw a plane about to land on her silver Toyota. Officials at Pease international Airport near Portsmouth guided her to safety.

Better watch out for those low flying planes, lady!

Terre Haute, IN: Three men and three women at an Indiana prison have been charged with sneaking through a hole in the ceiling to have sex with each other. Having found a security camera blind spot, the inmates would climb into the ceiling, drink homemade prison wine, play cards and do the wild thing.

Sounds like their own little highway to heaven, doesn't it.

Queens, NY: A bubble-gum bandit bit off more than he could chew recently when he was arrested and sent to jail for swiping almost a dozen packages of gum from a Queens store. William Rouse, 47, was caught on a surveillance camera pilfering gum from a K-Mart. A security guard grabbed him at the front door and found 54 packs of bubble gum stuffed in his bag. The loot was worth $172. This was in November 2008. In July 2008 Rouse had been arrested at a Queens' BJ's Wholesale Club trying to walk out of the store with 25 packs of gum stuffed in his beach bag. Upon being arrested for that heist Rouse bragged to the arresting officer that, "This place is a gold mine!"

Sounds like this crook needs gum control.

Yavapai, AZ; Courtroom police arrested an Arizona lawyer. Why? Because he gave his shackled client a piece of candy. Court officers in Yavapai told Damon Rossi,38, not to feed his client the sweets. Rossi asked the courtroom cops, "What are you going to do, arrest me?" They did just that, two days later at his Prescott Valley home.

How silly...What a waste of public money.

Beverly Hills, CA: Dr. Craig Alan Bittner, a Beverly Hills liposuction doctor turned the fat he removed from patients into biodiesel fuel that propelled his Ford SUV and his girlfriend's Lincoln Navigator. Problem is, it's illegal in California to use human medical waste to power vehicles. Dr. Bittner is being investigated by the state Department of Health.

They must have a law against everything in California. Wonder who thought of this one?

Weird Criminal Law Stories

Finally, some of Professor Birdsong's favorite weird stories from 2008:

Portland, OR: Tremayne Durham, 36, was recently sentenced to life in prison with the chance for parole after thirty years. Durham was sentenced for the murder of Adam Calbreath over a business deal that had gone bad. Instead of going to trial Durham availed himself of a very unusual plea deal offered by the prosecutor. He had sat in jail almost two years awaiting trial and missed the greasy food he liked to eat. So, when the prosecutor offered him a fast food buffet in exchange for his guilty plea Durham admitted he had shot Calbreath. His buffet deal included gorging himself on KFC and Popeye's chicken, mashed potatoes, coleslaw, carrot cake, a pizza, two calzones, lasagna and ice cream. The judge signed off on the plea deal and Durham downed the food at two settings. Cost to the Oregon taxpayers was only $41.70. A murder trial would have cost the state $4,000.

That is one way to take a bite out of crime isn't it?

Pittsburgh, PA: Police report that Thomas Jones siphoned off more than $40,000 of gasoline from his ex-boss – by swiping a company gas card and using it to buy 11,000 gallons of gas for himself and others. Jones was arrested in mid July after his former boss at BW Wholesale Florist, Mike Ulrich, caught him in the act. Ulrich stated that after he reported Jones's $43,695.16 in fraudulent fill ups, he spotted Jones gassing up again – and delivered him to the police.

Jones must have driven one heckuva big SUV!

Denton, TX: What a weird and weird family reunion! Stephanie Ramirez was working in a pizza parlor in Denton, when a robber wearing a wig and sunglasses barged in and demanded cash. As Rameriz took money from the register a coworker tackled the robber knocking off his disguise – and revealing that the robber was Rameriz's father. Police say they do not think that Rameriz herself was in on the robbery.

…HHHHmmmmmm… but we are still mighty suspicious about that.

Rhode Island: Pictures from social networking web sites are cropping up in court. Online photos tripped up Joshua Lipton, a 20 year old college junior after he was charged in a drunken driving crash that seriously injured a woman. Two weeks after his arrest, he attended a Halloween party dressed as a prisoner. The photos were later posted on Facebook. Prosecutor Jay Sullivan used the photos to paint Lipton as an unrepentant partier living it up while his victim suffered in the hospital. The judge found the photos depraved and sentenced Lipton to two years in prison.

Ouch!

Cookeville, TN: Police recently arrested a one wheeled motorcycle dare devil. Officers said a 29 year old man popped a 400 yard wheelie on his motorcycle. The offense drew a reckless driving arrest.

Was that a motorcycle or a "donor"-cycle he was riding?

Bronx, NY: A combination Subway Sandwich shop and stripper business was recently shut down. Anthony "Cousin Vinny" Agnello ran afoul of a trademark lawsuit for offering Subway's signature 6 foot sandwiches – as well as Subway wrappers, bags and menus in his X rated deli. Agnello, 48, had sent out fliers promising customers free fountain sodas and $5 foot long subs alongside "six hours of nonstop, hardcore, live action from some of the most beautiful young ladies who have ever chosen to take their clothes off in public." A federal judge ordered him to stop using the trademarked goods in his skin scheme and forced him to pay more than $12,000 for the chain's legal fees. After the court's ruling a disappointed Agnello said, "The money in stripping isn't as profitable as it used to be. This Subway was my golden parachute."

It occurs to us that it just does not seem that Subway sandwiches and naked women would go well together.

Manhattan, NY: Robert Williams, described by prosecutors at his sentencing as a "deranged fiend" who kidnapped, raped, brutally tortured and nearly murdered a Columbia University graduate journalism student in 2007, was sentenced on July 24, 2008 to 422 years in prison. The sentence was the maximum number of years allowed by New York law. His victim was not in court at the sentencing. She wrote to prosecutors stating that she was "afraid to go outside." The victim narrowly survived her ordeal of being kidnapped, raped, sliced with a butcher knife, scalded with boiling water, drugged to the brink of death, had her lips Krazy glued together and then left for dead tied to her burning living room couch. Williams attempted to opt out of the sentencing hearing but was carried into the hearing by six helmeted shield carrying state court officers. Williams had already spent most of his adult life in prison.

Prison is where Williams belongs and he made sure he would get back there!

Cookeville, TN: From the "worst get away ever" file: Three men stole a recliner from a Goodwill store in Cookeville, threw it in the back of their pickup truck and tried to speed off, but the vehicle was out of gas and it stalled in the parking lot. Police found the truck, the recliner and the perpetrators in the middle of their own personal gas crisis.

It's not the kind of gas crisis most of us have!

Colorado: A man posing as a "porn inspector" tried to get the owners of an xxx-rated video shop to give him free videos, claiming he had to make sure performers were not under age. Of course, the local police when contacted by the video shop said they do not have a porn inspector.

Where is Inspector Gadget when you need him?

Pennsylvania: An 85 year old woman calmly walked past a burglar in her house, got her pistol, and ordered him to call police. He did so. Leda Smith said, "I just walked right past him to the bedroom and got my gun and said what are you doing in my house?"

Remember young blood -- don't mess with granny!

Burrillville, RI: A town councilor got more than he bargained for when he won a used police cruiser at an auction. Kevin Blais bought the 2004 Crown Victoria in an online auction from the Hartford, Conn., Public Works Department, and found a bag of cocaine inside. Blais speculates a suspect stuffed the drugs through a seat crack to prevent cops from finding it.

Your police, working for you.

Providence, RI: This undercover cop car obviously wasn't used for a K-9 unit. If it had, perhaps police would have been able to sniff out that the seized vehicle they had been using since 2000 had a half pound of cocaine hidden in the dashboard. Deputy Police Chief Paul Kennedy admitted that sometimes officers do "miss stuff" when searching contraband vehicles.

Must be the beautiful Rhode Island scenery....

Charleston, WV: Policed arrested a man who tried to rob a video store with an empty cheesecake box. Paul Parrish II, 43, of Charleston placed the box on the counter of the Movie Gallery with a note that said it contained a bomb. The clerk refused to give Parish any money and Parish ran out of the store. He was soon arrested and told police he needed money for gas and cigarettes.

Yep, its hard times all over.

Saratoga Springs, NY: Calvin Morett, a 19-year-old high school student was cited for disorderly conduct. His conduct? He showed up at his high school graduation dressed as a 6-foot penis. Officials allegedly reported that Morett went to court where he stood erect, manned up and pleaded guilty to the charge. For his punishment he was ordered to write a letter of apology to his school.

Not a very stiff punishment we would say!

South Carolina: A 31-year-old man, John Montgomery, tried to steal a monkey from an animal park but when the little monkey fought back, the thief settled for a bear cub instead. Montgomery then put the cub on display at a truck stop where he charged people $1 to pet it. He was charged with burglary.

Yep, it truly is hard times all over!!

Switzerland: No one was arrested, but thank God it wasn't real. A giant inflatable replica of dog poo blew away from an outdoor art exhibition in Switzerland, tearing down power lines and damaging homes in its path. The house sized replica turd, was ultimately corralled and brought back to the exhibition.

Who flung poo?

New Jersey: A 20 year old New Jersey woman who got behind the wheel while drunk, and then fled the scene after smashing her car into a utility pole, was caught by police who tracked her using personal papers left at the crash scene, police said. However, before she could be arrested for the smashup, the unidentified woman crashed into a stone wall about two miles from the original accident.

She should have been driving a bumper car!

Manhattan, NY: A cross-dressing bank robber donned a wig, makeup and women's clothing to throw police off the scent. Yet, he got caught because he could not disguise his large nose. Samuel Manoharan, 31,of North

Bergen, New Jersey, was arrested as a suspect in five bank robberies in Manhattan and Brooklyn because police were able to clearly identify him from his profile taken by bank surveillance cameras – namely his nose, sources said. "He has very distinguishable features – a very large nose. His wig couldn't cover his nose," said a police source.

Perhaps this is what is meant by sniffing out crime.

New York, NY: A cross dressing man snatched a purse from a 74 year old woman, but left behind a strange clue -- a condom filled with water that he had been using as a fake breast. The suspect, clad in a short denim skirt and black tube top, fled the scene in a car with two other transvestites. Police are checking the condom for fingerprint and DNA evidence.

Would you say it was a B cup or a C cup sized condom?

Minnesota: Minnesota police arrested a trio of teens suspected of breaking into a vending machine by following a trail of Cheetos dust back to their home. When found, the teens were covered in a thin layer of orange dust.

We know...it was really Chester Cheetah that did it.

Winsted, CT: A Pup Tent Pervert? A rapist and high risk sex offender in Connecticut was arrested after he pitched a tent and lured children inside with candy and ice cream. Robert Logan, 34, a registered sex offender from Arkansas was charged with fourth degree sexual assault and breach of peace. Police say Logan offered candy, ice cream and money to several children one July weekend after pitching a tent at the edge of a parking lot behind an apartment building. A 7 year old told her parents that Logan "pulled her bathing suit away from her bottom and looked at her bottom. The parents reported this to police. Logan denies anything inappropriate. Logan sits in jail with his bond set at $125,000.

Yep, jail is where he belongs.

Mobile, AL: Police believe a body found in a small time evangelist's home freezer is his wife and a mother of eight children. Police arrested him on a murder charges as he preached at a southern Alabama church. Anthony Hopkins, 37, was being held in jail awaiting a bond hearing. Police said no one reported 36-year-old Arletha Hopkins missing, even though she had not been heard from in three years. The body was discovered in a freezer in a utility room during a police search of the home.

Eight children and nobody missed her! Sounds mighty suspicious…

Indiana: This one is about a new cop who got off on the wrong foot. Tim Pochron had been on the job for only 29 minutes during his first day on the police force when he wrecked his police car. In his defense, the other driver who crashed into him tested positive for drugs and was arrested.

Maybe, Pochron needs to find a less dangerous line of work.

OHIO: An Ohio murderer is trying to avoid being executed by claiming he is so fat, it would be difficult to find a vein to give him a lethal injection. Richard Cooey, who at 5 foot 7 tips the scales at 267 pounds is scheduled to die October 14, 2008.

Professor Birdsong thinks the prison's head chef was too good to Cooey.

###

About the Author

Professor Birdsong received his J.D. from the Harvard Law School and his B.A. from Howard University. He teaches law in Orlando, Florida.

After graduation from law school he worked four years at the law firm of Baker Hostetler. He then entered into a varied and distinguished career in government service. He served as a diplomat with the U.S. State Department with various postings in Nigeria, Germany and the Bahamas.

Professor Birdsong later served as a federal prosecutor. After leaving government service, and before he began teaching, Professor Birdsong was in private law practice in Washington, D.C.

www.BirdsongsLaw.com

lbirdsong@barry.edu

Ordering Information

New books coming soon!

Dear Reader,

If you liked this book, I would greatly appreciate you writing me a review on Amazon or any other book site.

I look forward to sharing more funny stories with you in future books.

Thank you, I really appreciate your help.

Regards,

Professor Birdsong

Winghurst Publications
1969 S. Alafaya Trail / Suite 303
Orlando, FL 32828-8732
www.BirdsongsLaw.com
lbirdsong@barry.edu

Other books by Professor Birdsong:

* Professor Birdsong's 147 Dumbest Criminal Stories: Florida.

* 177 Dumbest Criminal Stories – International.

* Professor Birdsong's 157 Dumbest Criminal Stories.

* Professor Birdsong's Weird Criminal Law Stories.

* Professor Birdsong's "365" Weird Criminal Law Stories for Every Day of the Year.

* Professor Birdsong's Weird Criminal Law Stories, Volume 2: Stories From Around the States and Abroad.

* Professor Birdsong's Weird Criminal Law Stories, Volume 3: Stories from New York City and the East Coast.

* Professor Birdsong's Weird Criminal Law Stories - Volume 4: Stories from the Midwest.

* Professor Birdsong's Weird Criminal Law Stories, Volume 5: Stories from Way Out West.

* Professor Birdsong's Weird Criminal Law Stories - Volume 6: Women in Trouble.

* Professor Birdsong's Weird Criminal Law - Volume 6: Women in Trouble!

* Immigration: Obama must act now!

* Professor Birdsong's 77 Dumbest Criminal Stories.

* Professor Birdsong's Dumbest: Thugs, Thieves, and Rogues.

* Professor Birdsong's LAW SCHOOL GUIDE: Techniques for Choosing, and Applying to Law School.

Weird Criminal Law Stories